from the Negro Psalmist to the Nappy-Headed Christ
Psalms, Laments, & Songs
poetry for the 21st Century Negro

Second Edition

from the Negro Psalmist to the Nappy-Headed Christ
Psalms, Laments, & Songs
poetry for the 21st Century Negro

Helen Kamilah Amon Bailey

Helen Kamilah Amon Bailey
PO Box 775005
Saint Louis, MO 63177

ISBN: 9798308067900

Third Printed Edition.

Independently published.

author's photo: Alex Don Media Group

these words are dedicated to the particularly melanated peoples of the global majority

Table of Contents

Contents cont.

preface

we see that in the beginning God spoke. to speak is to create. the Bible describes God's word as living & active, sharper than a double-edged blade; so sharp, in fact, it can separate your soul from your spirit. it also says that God's words are able to discern the thoughts and intentions of the heart.

& greater things are we able to do
John 14:12-14

read these words aloud & watch them come to life
read these words aloud & feel your heart come alive

Psalms

/sä(l)m/
a sacred hymn or song; a poem; a prayer

G.U.U.F.

unity barely exists
& people from many sides take advantage
to exploit The People

God, how can the veil be removed again?
how can truth win out?
when will darkness be brought to the light?

we want to be free. all people want to be free.

beauty in the breakdown

when your spirit hovered over
the water
while the abyss thrived and grew
you saw me

       you knew me

you beckoned my soul to fill an earthen vessel

do we not say that distance fills the heart
with fondness?

how is it then that once separated from you
in Heaven my fondness grew stale?

with dominion over the land & paradise at
our feet still we fell prey.

still we fall prey & yet won't pray

the potential of the world
waiting for our voices yet we have fallen short

knowledge

I understand less as I live.
each fabric of knowledge I sew
together
leads me away from truth.
your truth that transcends
Earth & sky,
       life & death,
            time & space—
it escapes me as I warm my life with
the guilt of knowledge.

for what good is knowledge if it
separates me from the human-ness of humanity?
you crafted our mortal bodies from the very
ground you spoke into existence—how is it that we
levitate above it only to conclude there is no God in
Heaven?
connect us back to the roots of the beginning:
when humanity was a song in the beak of a cardinal;
when love was a whisper in the wind.

inadequate praise

You, for whom time does not exist,
for whom yesterday is today is tomorrow.
You, who lavish love on those who are true.
thank you for your love
I feel your love with the passage of time,
in every moment of joy,
in every death that I see.

You are the One God who gave me a mind to see,
an understanding of spiritual matters & a heart to suffer.

it pleases my heart to know you are there.
it comforts my soul that you care for me.
in the end, following your voice will be
all that really mattered.

You, God, are who can do anything, everything—
you're healing across the Diaspora, across the world.

my praise is inadequate.
you know this yet accept me because of who are you.
who am I to you but a line in your palm?

Hana

God is not a man that He would lie,
nor a woman that She would
allow you to speak on her name
(blaspheme) with no consequence.

how then, Saints of God, is it that
you come to Her with your hands
out, no sacrifice in sight?

how can it be, Beloved, that you
claim to know Him, but won't fast
in order to train your mind, body,
& soul?

this is folly!

the God of Heaven deceived by
your deceptive words & meaningless
gestures? HELLO? this is not the truth.

God is not a woman that He would
feign ignorance when sin is committed;
nor is God a man that She would soften
a blow to spare your feelings.

feel this blow, you scorned of our faith,
usurpers of the Gospel for power &
profit, who rape & steal, murder &
displace in the name of Yeshua the
Lion of Judah.

truth hidden & buried beneath lies
will shine brighter than the light of
day when revealed. or have you
forgotten that things done in deep
dark places always surface at high tide
in the end?!

and it is the end for those
who merely claim the name of God,
who fabricate an anointing with
olive oil kept in clear vessels.

we

your words are a mirror for life.
I read them silently to myself and I
see only the reflection of others.
silence brings judgment
& for judgment, your words easily fan a flame.

yet when I read your words and speak them
into the air I see myself.
your words create life and love;
when I hear them my soul is filled.

& so it is with my own words. the *Spirit
of America* seeks to destroy all that you
placed inside me. in your image, my words are spells
that alter the very fabric of the air surrounding me.
guided by your spirit my words break strongholds.
resting within you my words dismantle the lies
& deceptions of colonization & settlement.

who can I run to?
where can I hide?
the mountains & hills where we once
found solace have been desecrated and
converted into monuments of apartheid,
graven images of the unreal & unclean.

those who seek to silence us have weaponized
your words. they seek to, themselves, put the
first in last place.

how will you defend? we seek *reparation*.
we seek Peace but if we cannot find her we choose violence.

come, Holy One.

fulfill your word.

we await you,

the God of Emmett, Breonna & Huey.

seed of Abraham

who hath more nations than the Negro?
perhaps the ocean's depths,,,

yet

maybe the stars in all their clusters & galaxies.

was it not the seed of Abram made Abraham
that was blessed to multiply & fill the earth
as the sand fills the shores of the sea?

remember the creation of your likeness, O God.
bless your firstborn & let other nations be
blessed because we are blessed.

return your children of the sun to their rightful
places as stewards & shepherds of your Earthly
realm.

give us the strength to fight for justice & the
grace to forgive once reconciliation is complete.

spin the block

you've sent your prophets to liberate & still here we remain—
cut off, exiled, stripped of our languages and cultures.
yesterday a man running and yelling for his friend was
pierced with lead and killed in the street.

where is our peace and refuge? even with our hands raised
in surrender to you they still our bodies with a flash of steel.

our only crime is life yet they cut off our futures with the
flick of a wrist. they leave us naked in the street, beat
our dead flesh with sticks, then scandalize our names.

our labor is stolen in exchange for our lives, otherwise
more profitable to them dead than free, they erase
& wash all traces of our ancestry, of our history.

we pray to you, the God of our ancestors.
the God of Medger, Sandra, & Dolph

ball till they fall

who will we blame when the usurpers ruin the
earth you created? the waters rise without your say.
the forests disappear under ax, fire, & siege.
while your people shout, "Enough!," our words
remain unheard.

send your holy one bent on destruction, the
pestilence is not enough. the structured regime
has set its face against us. destroy it. we beg of
you. if the wicked are truly like chaff then blow
them away.

your enemies have not kissed your
son as commanded. they stripped him, shaved
his head, & gave him the name of a son of Babylon.
may their teeth shatter with each swallow of
oppression, each devoured morsel of suppression.

those with bared teeth behind masks of smiles
masquerade themselves as Sons while those who
were given the bread of adversity are trapped in
darkness & depravity.

while we may be put away to die we yet live & thrive
because of your mighty hand. we continue to be the
children of God though you were removed from the
genealogies of our ancestors.

rejoice, melanated tribes, for God has not
abandoned you. though unrecognizable for a time the
Light has again been revealed.

what was forbidden in captivity has been restored.
what was called ugly is now beautiful again.
divination is again the wisdom of the divine.
our urim & thummin have been found, shuffled,
& spread on a table.

we tear off the clothing of shame like King Josiah
when the law was rediscovered. fashion us new garments
made with the light of Heaven that our god-likeness
might shine &
              blind &
                    slay

the clearing: quiet place

when sorrow attempts to crush my head
from within I have to make a quick escape
run
run far away to my quiet place
I inhale the trouble of the day & blow it
out again—back to hell where it belongs

when capitalism attempts to drain the
life within me, I have to take a break &
run
run far away to my quiet place
I inhale the sorrows of the day & blow
them out again to join the other pollutants

when facing life as it is overwhelms my
psyche, I have to pour out my heart to
Spirit, so I
run
run far away to my quiet place
I inhale the inconveniences of the day &
blow them out again, they have no place
in my mind's eye

the longer I'm here the more relaxed I
feel; the longer I breathe deeply the more
peace surrounds me

where are the voices lamenting
beforehand who would not give me a
moment's peace? they are silent for my
quiet place is a fortress, a refuge of
tranquility

being quiet leads to a clear mind,
leads to hearing from Spirit.
when silence surrounds me, my mind is at ease

what does God fear?

what do you fear, you inhabitants
of the Diaspora?
you fear death yet die
you fear change yet what has remained the same?

whom do you fear, ethereally rhythmic people?!
you fear yourselves for you are powerful beyond measure
you fear them yet they covet who you are

where do you look for the salvation you fear
will not come, Negro people of the Earth?
you must look to the hills
you must look to yourselves

lament & cry out to God, your maker,
you inhabitants of the Diaspora!

God fears neither tears nor grief & sorrow

laugh & smile when you sing of God's
goodness, all who are blessed with the
rhythm of the Earth!

God fears neither melanin nor naps & kinks

twist & shout, heel toe & swag your praises
to the God of Justice, all Negro peoples the
world over!

God fears neither change nor protest & revolution

which craft?

for the ones mislabeled Jezebel—

sing out all you heaux & praise God in Heaven!
sing & rejoice you heaux, Jehovah Mekoddishkem has
come to redeem you. you are precious to God, beautiful
child. your redeemer says,

"Come. Rejoice & do not weep
for your sacrifice has not been overlooked. Your dedication
to me through your lovers will be counted to you as
righteousness for I am the God of Rahab who without
regard for her own person & endangering the lives of her
relatives shielded My People & saved them."

"Sit at my feet & consider those who sentence you to
hell ablaze, those for whom scarlet could not measure
the depth of their sin."

"Surrender the fruit of your garden to me, unrivaled
child so bare. Allow the dew of the dawn to wash you
anew.

"Here with me & this cloud of witnesses, you are
free to roam & heal whomsoever you might.

"Leave your pursuers to me.

"I will love you as a poor man loves his only child
& caresses him or puts a kiss on her head. Be mine
again. Sing & dance your spells before me, children
of Zion. I will hear you. I will grant your desire to see
me face-to-face, as I am."

rejoice,
all you heaux,
your Triumph has come.

with the patience of Job

there is no rival to the One God of all;
the origin of our spiritual being,
the creator of our mortal bodies.

God, you are glorious—from everlasting to everlasting.
truly your heart captivates to the utmost
truly your cause of righteousness & justice are
good and worthy of implementation.

You hear me cry out in agony for you to save us,
that we will repent;
each one to their own, faithfully
each one to the One.

if one day is like a thousand to you then tell us
how long have we suffered under the light of
Heaven's source? would you now say there is
more we must endure past one hundred seven
million four hundred sixty thousand days
before your very eyes?

I long for the time you will go out before us in battle
& give us victory before the faces of our enemies.
while I sit longing, I pray that time is now...

you People

rising up from the ashes
again & again
a phoenix is born to fan
the flames in the hearts
of The People

look & see, you People!
our oppressors have no
power. they have only lies,
while our power they deny.
they have barbarized our
passion for their personal profit

wake up, you People!
not to the narratives developed
by the lazy & incompetent, who
seek to delegitimize The People
for clout & swift gain, who peddle
spiritual matters they cannot
comprehend

awaken to the truth, you People!
the truth of your heritage, the truth
of your ancestry! allow it to fill
your mind & belly as one allows
the leaf of leisure to fill the lungs
& saturate the body

lock in with the fortitude &
discernment of your ancestors
find peace in solitude, wisdom
in the presence of trusted
advisors.

impiety

they herald your name in the street
with thunderous voices,

>
> "Behold the King comes who will
> find you unworthy and treat
> you to hell!"

yet, in the still of day you whisper
reminders of love to your holy ones—
those who hear and act upon your word.

away with you who would scoff at God's
nearness to those who suffer needlessly under
the light of the sun, under the watchful eyes
of the mockers of God.

away & give your life recklessly to the crop of
the field painted neatly with stars and stripes—
crops cannot save you. none but God alone is
willing to forfeit eternity to pluck you from the
depth of the unending abyss.

"Naught but your full heart will satisfy me," says
The God of Order, The Arbiter of Justice.
"Surrender your hate and your despair. Though
you were not chosen I care for you. Remember
not the rejection you felt but sit with me and
listen. Remember me, for though you are not
mine I am yours."

we cry out to you, God. asè and amen.

freedom

the days of rejoicing seem distant in my eyes
days filled with laughter, singing, dancing...
where are you now, God of my life?
fires burn in the street and as we fill our lungs
with smoke from the reed of resistance we
exhale something new:
awakening
an old beat with a new sound.

those gathered in the road to watch the blaze
mock & shout at us,
whose stifled frustrations of
impoverishment can only be articulated by
flames.
"We are God," they declare, not understanding
that the lording of power & hoarding of resources
are trademarks of the wicked & the antichrists.

oh, where are you now, God of my death?
do not any longer keep your hand from us.
seize our hearts again
in triumph not desperation,
in victory not defeat,
in joy not sorrow.

vindicate us.

let us return to you not as defeated prodigals
but as warriors returning from captive battle with honor.
allow us the freedom to free ourselves by your
hand, allow our might to sustain us by your grace.

do you call this faithful?

I have yet to grasp humility so
I come to you as I am:
brokenhearted, alone,
crying for my Native Land

My God, My
God!

do you not move across the water
in the stillness of the day? do you
not speak out to us in answer for
when we pray?

where is the One who we know
exists outside of time? we ask
you to reverse the curse & free us
from all lies.

you are the God of old, the One
who makes breath become. you
are the One foretold, who will
break the chains of everyone.

imprisoned in my neighborhood,
I wait to see if you are faithful
come again, do a miracle here
so we know that you are able
to lift the burdens off our backs
& free our hearts from devastation.

I lay all my righteousness before
you though I have none to give.
teach us to love, teach us to give,
teach me to pray, teach me
to lament

your power & wisdom are all we need,
strength & progress are what we seek,
give us a reason to hope & breathe.
bring corrupt systems down to their
knees.

I seek to cry out to you on
behalf of all who are me.
I seek to tip your hand in
favor of justice on behalf
of those who look like me.

let Freedom ring true here again in
America, my native land, to
ETHIOPIA where Earth (we) began.
free us to be free indeed.
free us now, "give us, us free"

on behalf of all my
brethren I cry out to
you:

àṣẹ.

*an agreement or affirmation in Yoruba, similar to Amen, meaning "so shall it be" & the power to create what you speak. an invitation to rest here before moving on.

Lamentations

/ˌlamənˈtāsʜcən/
the passionate expression of grief or sorrow; an elegy or dirge; a prayer

good mourning?

I cry in the darkness of twilight only to be
cursed by my neighbor

I cry from the depths of my soul & I'm asked
to keep it down

when will my mourning turn to joy? how will
peace enter when chaos has the door of my heart
bolted shut?

how am I left out in the cold from my own home?

1919

singing for the sake of singing is a burden to me
now; there are no songs sung that capture the
ache of my heart.

I lack the faith of my ancestral kin who jumped
to their deaths from the bows of ships, who'd
crossed the 7 seas in arks of triumph & divine right.

I long to gather with the ancestors. maybe then
a song for the sake of music would heal the pain
of my heart.

how might it be if I gathered together with
my kin instead? would our hearts beat as one?
I hear no answer

I close my eyes to imagine a world where we never
separated, where a person like myself could lift up
their voice to sing & at once be met with a chorus of
voices singing in harmony.

were the song filled with the faith brought by our
dark past perhaps I could remove the glass from my
neck & join the proletariat. but alas, my treachery has
befallen upon me the fate of Judas.

speak through tears

born of the earth yet forced to disconnect
from its lifeforce. the way through which
salvation can come to all—coerced into silence.
even in our silence we are hunted & slaughtered.
even when we forgive, we are cast aside as transgressors.
God of all dominions, do not allow propaganda to
compel us to turn the other cheek. send relief & destroy
the scorn of the Earth who make a mockery of The
People from God. sever their hold the world over &
throw their descendants into confusion. let the darkness
of the abyss swallow their unrepentant souls.

abandon your prolonged judgement for we are weary

protego totalim

sing out to Heaven
cry aloud, for your freedoms are
laid bare on the chopping block

God without name belongs to you
demand the peace & prosperity
that is your birthright;

activate your ancestral protections,
People of the Sun.

cry out to God & lament, for the
Earth crumbles before your very
eyes. what belongs to you remains
at hand while you overdose on self-
indulgence & perish in sorrow

all whilst those who rule without
justice & without humility from
their left hands, who with their
right hands siphon the Earth of all
God called good— return her to the
second verse of the Orthodox Tewahedo,
the first verse of the Law of Moses.

arm yourselves for war, remembering
with whom you truly fight against.
arm yourselves accordingly
pray without ceasing.

sweet release

death is near, O God of my sorrow.
a life that ends is a life complete.
I long to be vindicated while my
eyes and heart yet fail. help me see you
face-to-face. give me the peace of
eternal life with you.

come soon, God of vengeance.
I am no foot soldier in your army;
my loyalties have been with the
enemy, rising through the ranks,
prolific in my assault against you.

come quickly, God of reciprocity; I
crave your justice. put an end to my
suffering and embrace me. show me the
blueprints for New Jerusalem. walk with me
again in the Valley of the Shadow of Death for
old times sake.

revisit the past with me &
justify the injustices endured by my
kindred that led me to fight against you.

with the wisdom you give I know
who & what destroyed my ancestors,
where, when & how it all went wrong.
I blame you because you can take it &
the wicked take the truth to be hard

please remove me from this torture chamber
release me from this unjust existence

nothing

it's no wonder you gaze upon me yet hide your face.
I am nothing.
You are all in all.

You are from morning to morning,
changing every moment while remaining the same.
I am from evening to evening,
changing every moment while forgetting the past.

what is dust that you make mention of it next to your name?

I, in my insignificant nothingness, dare to call on your
name for you've declared you loved me first.
do I not open the door of my heart to you because you
first knocked and wanted to see my face?

You are the One, existing before existence existed!
since you are the God who has freed many before and
more to come, I will trust that you have come to fulfill
your word.

the greatest gift—a fulfilled word.

& yet

what is it, my God, that fuels the rage within?

how will you extinguish it when justice does not
prevail on the Earth?

the wicked taunt us with the history of our oppression,
they ridicule & say that for 20 score years you did not
come & you will not come now.

you are sovereign over the wind, waves, & soil
over the mind, body, soul & spirit
come to our aid, O God.

crying out to you, my voice is carried away by the wind.
do you send the wind and my cries to the abyss?

your love feels far from me

are you not our God—able to change the tide
in a moment, able to pause the Earth's rotation?

my father's pleas you shut down with your might.
now it is I who calls out, "Violence! Please
save us from the grip of our enemies."

yet there is nothing. silence.

you alone are able to save...

you alone are able to heal...

you alone are faithful—

honor your word. come to our rescue.

lover's despair

when hearts become entangled in the watching of the night
you see and hear.
your love, however,
does not retreat.

our love created in the night is no match for yours yet
it fills me with much less fear.
must a rendezvous under the shadow of moonlight
comfort my heart more than you?

where are you when I cry alone at night?
when the light of my eye dims to darkness where can I find
you? have you not forsaken your loved ones?

show me, again, to connect with you
in the stillness of darkness.
give an ear to the cry of my heart
longing for truth.
you know that even in despair
my desire is for you.

manufactured joy & peace

you have limited my ability to function
as I'd like, so as the elixir of energy passes
through my lips I think of you.

this mind that you gave me no longer
computes as it ought so I allow the plume
from the mellow leaf to fill my lungs.

I sip joy and toke peace.

another day has begun and I did not
seek you when you could be found.

my body—created to mimic you—fails.

I rely on your spiritless creation to stimulate
the spirit within me, knowing that the spirit
within me longs to mature and grow.
instead of basking in the light of the
star, I turn my back.

redemption

we have traveled far & been brought low,
low enough to be tread upon like ash.
blessed be that out of ashes the
phoenix rises
sing & shout that the phoenix can be
utterly destroyed but not killed

we started from the bottom of their
registers & rose to top billing
now we're here at the bottom again,
clinging to life while losing consciousness

for their fear is our prison, their incompetence
is our death—give us strength to break free
from their devastation & still more strength.
take us by the still waters to rest & refresh
our hearts. be gentle with our wounds for we
have been beaten mercilessly, tormented
beyond recognition & left for dead.

revive us, God. show us again how the Earth
is your footstool. show us again what it means
for your train to fill the temple.

six nine one two

evil lives among us.
fallen angels in human flesh
walk the streets armed for war.

come, walk among us again though
the cool of the day vanishes under
the ever-scorching sun.

come, breathe in the lacrimator but
do not allow it to blind you to
our suffering.

come, feel the flesh laid bare by baton
rounds called harmless yet filled
with lead.

are these not the bones formed by you
in our mother's wombs?

make it make sense, O God!

we rot from within in this accursed land

come, dine with us & taste the bane
of death added to the food in our cities.

come, drink with us from poisoned
riverways with cups fashioned of poverty.

come, be intimate with us & we'll show you
how come our lovers all leave.

have you not heard that our children are
stolen & made to live with the unclean
while our mothers are labeled hypersexual
welfare queens & our fathers are left for dead
in rooms that measure 6 by 9 by 12?

we implore you to come

a time to heal

they celebrate in churches & cathedrals—
there is laughing & rejoicing for the time that is.
yet the love of God cannot be found in their midst.

the love of God cannot be found in their charities & food drives.
the love of God cannot be found in their children's homes nor is
the love of God found in their shelter.
will you forever make the cause of the widow & orphan,
the displaced & downtrodden your annuities?

a soul-home without repentance cannot contain the love of God

for now, there may be much to smile & kiki about at your
galas & benefits where the love of God cannot be found.
please do remember the time that is to come;
the time to come will not be a celebrated thing.

the haunches you throw in your merry circles is a far cry from
the ring shout of old. oh, that you would be...forreal with the God
of Heaven who calls you softly atop a hill just miles from home,
praying to see your face again, hopefully anticipating your return.

there is nothing stopping you from
calling a solemn assembly,
coordinating a tearing of clothes &
adornment of ash in repentance to
the One of all, the One with neither beginning nor end.

good grief, unmeasured

peace cannot simply be a thought or a whisper
hashtags cannot convey the urgency with which we must address the evils
of today:
fascism,
slavery,
occupation.
colonization.
mere words
as even the bloodstained fabric of this god-adulterated society crumbles to
nothing

God, where are you?
you've abandoned your people the world over, given victory to those who
commit, ignore, & profit from genocide under the light of the sun, boldly
and bare-faced with outstretched hands demanding more, presenting
themselves as victims of their own injustices.

how can we say you are good?
you require ritual & sacrifice, prayer & fasting? PLEASE. you require
nothing for you do nothing. the "Christians" do nothing but incur wrath &
blaspheme, disenfranchise & displace, destroy & deplete the entirety of
your creation.

what good is Heaven when Earth kills the soul? how is it that you ask for
more when you've allowed everything to be taken away with no semblance
of hope of their return? even our very breath is confiscated & used in a lie
our children do not rest safely in the safety you promised
our mothers & fathers are lawfully held under unjust laws.

where is the God who carries out vengeance on behalf of those who
believe?
just as even you came to despise the blood of bulls & goats, we, too, are
tired of insignificant retroactive justice. we require justice now, God.

terrify & kill the terror in one fell swoop. blind those who turn their eyes
toward our plight yet do less than enough. amputate the limbs of those
who extend their hands on our behalf only to pull back & bite their
thumbs. eviscerate those guilty of bloodlust for generations past who cheer
for & suppress our cries for help. they rejoice & celebrate the evil works of
their hands. they boast of their depravity & enlist the cooperation of the
foolish to reproduce themselves.

while the outwardly righteous inwardly decaying roam free with power we
will not say that God is good.

suffer not the children

there is no justification for injustice, neither on Earth nor in Heaven.

where are those who say they love God more than the rest?
they are shouting at the gate, "come out, let us abuse your children!"

& the ones who pray aloud in quiet places, what has become of them?
they stand at the door while your children are gunned down, slaughtered.

where are the people who have avowed their lives to our father in Heaven?
their nakedness is laid bare, burying their flesh into the backs of these little
ones.

hypocrites! scoffers!

they feign fear while wreaking unholy havoc on the least of these. they are
who the prophets warned you about—the antichrists.

the goodness of God has been misconstrued as acceptance &
they waste what time they have left defending their evil deeds.
they convince you to go along with their debasement to your detriment.
they will not stand in the judgment or in the congregation of the righteous.
they shall perish for they are already perishing.
they stifle the light for their eternity is darkness though they imagine it to
be the City of God.

woe to all who would cause little children to suffer under the light of the
sun, who would steal their bread in order for their own tables to overflow.

heed the parable of Nathan & repent—turn away from evil & do what is
good!

can those who are beset to do evil from generations past repent and turn
away as their guilt multiplies?

only God knows.

selah.

*a musical, liturgical, or literary pause** in Hebrew.
an invitation to rest here before moving on.

**this is one interpretation. meaning is debated among scholars.

Songs

/sông/

poetical composition; a prayer

reigning sun

you open my eyes to watch your sun rise

you open my eyes again when your sun sets

from the first light to the last you watch

& reign

a song for Solomon

between spring & fall you transform into
another beautiful hue, King. as we dance
& vibe in the sunlight the Spirit reflects
around us illuminating the brilliance of
your smile

collaborate with me, my love, on the song
of our lives. our lovers celebrate for we
have chosen one another. take me to the
throne of grace upon the bed of our love

take me to the beautiful countryside where
the birds cry aloud in worship, where the
men plow fields & expect no harvest. allow
our embrace to echo through time as we
exchange energy, combine & heal

your fingers softly fall down my face as
our eyes close & we fall into one another's
embrace. our caramel chocolate swirl
hurricanes into a tidal wave

as we catch our breath an offering of praise
wells up inside me & overcome by the
generosity & graciousness of life Mary's
praise from Luke forms on my lips and I
sing aloud...

alas, my love, the night has come. let
us sleep & rise to find our dreams
come true

the love poem

I loved you with my whole chest, even though I was envious of all the others who seemed to captivate you. I was jealous for your heart.

I loved you with my whole heart yet it irritated me how you refused to acknowledge me, so I blew up at you because it hurt me. I pretended to be indifferent to your indifference.

I loved you with every fiber of my being so I bragged to others that I knew you & loved you. I was satisfied with their misunderstanding of my relationship with you.

I loved you more than I loved myself, therefore neither of us could take shelter under its banner. I diminished myself in order for you to shine.

I have not been patient in the pruning process for I've selfishly insisted I knew the best path, though no path I chose led me to who I wanted you to be.

I could not believe the best for myself & I would not put my hope in truth's table. I delighted in extinguishing my own fire because kindness avoided me.

I failed myself & laid face down in defeat, arrogantly cursing & blaming everyone but myself, resentful that love seemed to resist my embrace.

on this, my final reflection, I see I have never loved before;
I created no love for myself, therefore none ever grew within me.

I loved you in the past tense, for it was never love at all.

By the Lake No 1

ache of my heart,

I would rather you attack than leave me here
in this retched state

loss of a lover or a child cannot compare,
though I have neither

pain takes me under the surface of its
moist embrace

it was done in the dark & there I hoped it
might stay:
blindingly bright for all to see but
not quite clearly

I have betrayed myself to the core of my
mortal body where joint & marrow separate

leave me here to wilt & wither. I will be cut
from the vine & blow away like chaff

before I am pruned, I will say to the vine, "I no
longer have need of you," & in my words
capture the very relief I desire—
an unending death

a hoodoo love story

sweet love of mine, how can I ever
hope to leave your side? when we
move as one life is transformed,
when we dance together the tide
changes. to separate from you is
to remove a measure of joy from
my cup.

sweet lover of mine, how sweetly
can I sing to you that would lead
you to forgive me? though my heart
does ache for you I cannot change
who I am, my love.
could I
would I
should I beg for forgiveness
knowing I will hurt you again?
release me from the vault of
your heart for I am no longer yours.

how can I betray my destiny for a
mere token of happiness, a one-up
over someone else? peace. peace
that doesn't make sense is far
superior to trinkets of love.

I will yet trust in God to renew &
replace what destiny has stolen
from us. after transitioning into
the sun I will find you & we will
run together for eternity.

the audacity of survival

in this space hope is safe. it waits.
it yearns. it lies in wait for the future.
survival occurs in each second &
for this your name is spoken in
vain. the constant cycling exhausts
the soul:
love
hate
despair
rage
understanding
forgiveness
love
hate

with neither held nor bated breath

we say that love is one thing & that
it is not another. I've nearly suffocated
waiting for the timing of another.

my future is determined by the hand
of my God, therefore I will no longer
wait with held nor bated breath.

let us now say that love is God & God's
breath gives life & life is all I need. for
now all is illuminated by the light of hope
in God.

we say that God is not & that is why
we look for love.

pillar forlorn

perfect poetry is all I ever hope to ever write
sometimes I feel like I'm not allowed to be joyful
the moment I feel like writing about happiness I think
of the longing in my heart to kill loneliness in the world
it distracts me from my purpose, getting lost in the
shadows of the day, complaining of the chill

yet could that be my mission here?
to sacrifice the joy in my heart so that you can feel loneliness?
to taste, for you, the depth of sorrow that comes from knowing
your love will never come true? your help may never come through?

my longing for your touch could steal a tear from the last dying bee
in this world neglected by our greediness & brokenness
how else can I explain to you having the power to save the future
yet looking back because I long for you?

please, God, if loneliness is my mission...— I'll do it for your Holiness.

Revolution Song

Holy are the ones who came here
        bound by hands & feet
Holy are those who stood on this land
        for countless centuries

Holy, Holy, Holy are our sacred traditions
        that God in Heaven says are good
           with cards & bones & leaves we
           divine with certainty, confirming
           with your Holy Ones

Hair clothed in rainbows, hands dyed indigo
        rice & cotton fields
Venerate those who came before us
        with faithful memory

Holy, Holy, Holy are our sacred traditions
        that God in Heaven says are good
           with lights & roots & gems we
           pray & expect to see the promises
           God made to us

Filled with love for the Negro Tribes of
        the Diaspora
We need to lift our voices & sing as one again that
        we will not be overcome

Holy, Holy, Holy are our sacred traditions
        that God in Heaven says are good
           with cards & bones & leaves we
           divine with certainly, confirming
           with your Holy Ones

Holy, Holy, Holy are our sacred traditions
        that God in Heaven says are good
           with lights & roots & gems we
           pray & expect to see the promises
           God makes to us

Holy, Holy, Holy are our sacred traditions
        that God in Heaven says are good
           with care & love & peace we
           heal our friends & family for
           truly all we have is us

maranatha.

*Aramaic prayer meaning, among other things, "Come, Lord Yeshua".
an invitation to rest & reflect here before moving on.

afterward

faith and belief in God are not things I've manufactured for myself. if I'm honest, God can be the inconvenient truth of my life. if I didn't have to believe I would not believe because that is so much easier. at times I have actively attempted to discard my faith in God, to live as though God didn't exist or at least not for me. it works every time, if only for a time. then out of nowhere, on a lonely day, when I'm too busy to eat, when no one is around, faith swirls up inside me and overcomes me to the point of tears. what am I left with? a repentant heart & an overwhelming feeling of love followed by a sense of peace. this is the gift of faith. it does not care what your desires are or what you're doing. God's gifts are non-refundable. now, the question becomes: what will I do with this faith?

well, for now, I've shared it with you. I pray we will lift each other's voices and sing the truth aloud.

outro

I had a lover
        once, twice
                perhaps thrice

he could not fathom the depth
of the sorrow of The People.
he could not comprehend my
heart & therefore his love
could not heal me

my mother's love heals me &
like the doe it protects my life
from the curse of hell that
slithers & seeks to constrict
my soul's glow

with boisterous breath I beseech The People:

        make God your mother again

SCRIPTURE TO CONSIDER:

1. Ecclesiastes 3:16 - 4:3

2. Isaiah 56:1 - 57:2

3. Habakkuk 1:12 - 2:4

4. Habakkuk 3:1-16

5. Habakkuk 3:17-19b

6. Matthew 5:33-46

7. Matthew 6:5-8

8. Matthew 22:34-40

9. Luke 18:1-30

10. Romans 2:12-16

11. Romans 8:18-29

12. Romans 14:19 – 15:13

13. 1 Corinthians 12:29 – 13:13

14. Colossians 2:1 – 3:16

15. 1 Peter 4:1-11

16. 1 John 2:17-19

17. Revelation 7:9-17

Translations Consulted:

Amplified Bible, Classic Edition

EasyEnglish Bible

First Nations Version

Good News Translation (US Version)

Holman Christian Standard

International Children's Bible

New American Standard Bible

The Passion Translation

World English Bible, American English Edition. without Strong's Numbers

Young's Literal Translation 1898

QUESTIONS TO CONSIDER:

1. What are the characteristics of love? What do those words & phrases mean individually?

2. What is the purpose of prayer?

3. What relationship do you have with prayer?

4. What similarities do you find between poetry & prayer?

5. What is the purpose of poetry?

6. When you pray what keeps you from asking for the desires of your heart?

7. How do you know when you've heard from God?

8. How do you distinguish the voice of God from the voices of others in your life?

9. What is the purpose of parables?

10. What similarities do you find between poetry & parables?

11. What will freedom cost you?

12. If you don't cry out for help, how will God come to your rescue?

13. What activities are you currently involved in that you believe will be counted to you as righteousness?

Appendix

Awkward Punctuation You May Have Noticed*—A Glossary of Sorts

lack of capital letters: like prayers, poems have no true beginning or end. for me, they always begin in the middle of a thought

"... —" there was more to this prayer that I chose to leave out. I also wanted to infer something; perhaps the request for it not to be so

"..?" there were more clauses to add to the question, but let's just get to hearing the answers

",,," dramatic pause or premature ending to a sentence (often seen as a misused ellipsis in casual writing)

"...'[text]" the beginning of the quoted text has been left out & the most familiar part of the quoted text has been reduced to a ' because/since it goes without saying

*listed punctuation may have been edited out of the final draft but remains glossary'd for your consideration.

More By

Helen Kamilah Amon Bailey

Have you ever had your heart ripped out of your chest? Ever been so completely devastated you considered leaving the faith?

Same.

How did you get there? How do you get back? Do you even want to go back?

Yeah, that's a tough one.

Don't worry. This devotional isn't to convince you to hold onto your faith. This devotional was written through tears and between panic attacks during the most difficult spring and summer of my life.

There is no agenda here except, maybe, that you can use this devotional as an excuse. An excuse to begin again and stand firm in your faith in the midst of hurt or disappointment. You don't need to be any particular denomination to read these pages.

I wrote this so I wouldn't die. I'm sharing it because I'm still alive.

Additional Suggested Reading

African Philosophy x Théophile Obenga

American Gods x Neil Gaiman

The Anti-War x Douglas Gwyn

Black Liturgies x Cole Arthur Riley

The Chronicles of Narnia x C.S. Lewis

David Walker's Appeal x David Walker

Holy Silence x J. Brent Bill

Hinds Feet on High Places x Hannah Hurnard

Letter from Birmingham Jail x Rev. Dr. Martin Luther King, Jr.

Mere Christianity x C.S. Lewis

The Message x Ta-Nehisi Coates

The Miseducation of the Negro x Carter Godwin Woodson

Mojo Workin' x Katrina Hazzard-Donald

On Tyranny x Timothy Snyder

The Opinions and Philosophies of Marcus Garvey x Amy Jacques Garvey

This Here Flesh x Cole Arthur Riley

Why We Can't Wait x Rev. Dr. Martin Luther King, Jr.

The Saint Louis Torchbearers 2

search for us on YouTube!

Passing the Flame to our Youth!

Vision
Providing the World with Youth Trained to Lead Now, Into the 22nd Century & BEYOND!

Mission
To train youth to serve in leadership roles among their peers, in their communities, & throughout the WORLD.

How We Accomplish Our Mission:
We accomplish our mission by training youth spiritually, physically, emotionally, cognitively, & socially. We assist youth in learning to use their Kinesthetic, Tactile, Auditory, Visual, Analytic, Intrapersonal & Interpersonal modalities through active participation in our programs:

Bible & Book Clubs, Service Learning,
Journal Writing, Swimming Lessons, Outdoor Education & Recreation,
Camping, Fishing, Biking, STEAM Lessons, Social-Emotional Development

WE BELIEVE
The world is a classroom.
Children have an inalienable right to develop cognitively, physically, emotionally, socially, & spiritually.
Leadership skills whether innate or acquired must be cultivated.
Children have the basic right to learn to be responsible, useful, & successful.
Inter-generational experiences are essential to positive leadership development.
Children must have ways to apply what they learn in practical ways.
Strong leaders create strong families & communities, thereby making the world a better place to live, work, & play.

CONSIDER DONATING TODAY!

P.O. Box 78007
St. Louis, MO
63178

Saint Louis Torchbearers 2
Scan to pay STorchbearers2

314-502-9122

We would love to hear how you received help from this book. To contact the author or book Helen to speak at your next event, scan here:

Blog: helenkabailey.wordpress.com

⟨○⟩: authoruhtee

Email Contact: admin@helenkabailey.com

about the author

Helen Kamilah Amon Bailey, daughter of Velma Gene Bailey & the late D.B. Amon, is a millennial and North Saint Louis native. Growing up under many different Christian denominations, Helen feels that her home lies with those who plainly & simply follow The Way. Committed to fostering an authentic relationship with God through Christ, Helen does not depend on established paradigms but on every word that proceeds from the heart of God. The world is changing day-by-day; Helen knows that God never changes and finds peace in that truth.

Habakkuk is Helen's Spirit Prophet.

Helen attends the St. Louis Friends Meeting with much regularity.

if you want to further this work:

authoruhtee

Serendipity

or

places in STL where one might run into the author

Lyrical THERAPY

WORDUP!
LIVE MUSIC POETRY COMEDY

#thuritis Thursday
Talk Show Open Mic

The Mantra House ॐ

The Lyrics & Laughs Interlude

Apex Lyricist Lounge

The Kre8ive Shop

violence

peace that surpasses all understanding is not a
commodity easily found. it comes from conscripted &
spontaneous periods of silence while listening, weeping,
praying, screaming. building yourself up in your most
holy faith sounds simple enough yet when you consider
that the building blocks are your very own blood,
sweat & tears, you may yet reconsider. the foundation
of your most holy faith must be composed of the fruit
of the spirit you've cultivated on the tree of your life.
having a working out of your salvation with fear &
trembling allows you to mix in the ashes of the fears
you've conquered through blind faith in the One.

where are the intimate lovers of God who feel the ring
of Heaven's call to abandon what was & be taught
again by the Spirit? how can we discern God's still
small voice trapped in the land of endless talking
heads? the splendor of Empire has duplicated the image
of the One into its American Gods.

very Roman. very Babylonian.

«Church_Name»
c/o «Leader_Title» «Leader_First_Name» «Leader_Last_Name»
«Church_Address»
«Church_City_State» «Church_Zip_Code»

To the Churches of North Saint Louis City & Abroad:

My name is Helen Bailey. In the poetry community, I'm known as authoruhtee (authority). I write prayers as poetry for revolution of the mind & heart. I grew up and live in the Jeff Vander Lou (JVL) neighborhood & although I was away from St. Louis for a long time, I returned to find the city had not changed very much, though, we were noticeably much further along in the Team 4 Plan. Since long-term city residents continue to be largely neglected & the city is being emptied of its history & the residents who are reminders of that history, I make this call to prayer. I hope we can lay aside every sin & weight, creed & doctrine, difference & grievance to come together and reconstruct the fabric of Saint Louis City through the transformative power of prayer with action.

I hope we can agree that while laws and politicians may be well & good, there are some things only God in Heaven can create and maintain. There is no one coming to rescue us because we ourselves are the help and hope we've been waiting for. I hope & request that you will join me in petitioning Heaven with the enclosed prayer by reading it aloud when you assemble together with congregants during worship service and in gatherings with family, friends & neighbors, whether celebrating or lamenting.

Freedom cannot simply be a thought or a whisper; let us lift our voices up to Heaven as the Hebrews in Exodus 2:23. Let us speak of our hope to one another as those in Malachi 3:16. Let us cry out to God with great expectation along with anticipation that those who have endured systemic inequality, generational trauma, & acts of racism will not only survive but thrive in peace.

Your Friend in the Truth,

Helen Kamilah Amon Bailey

authoruhtee
Helen Kamilah Amon Bailey
daughter of
Velma Gene Bailey
& the late D.B. Amon

Please address written responses to:
Good Light Coaching & Consulting, LLC
P.O. Box 775005   OR   admin@helenkabailey.com
St. Louis, MO 63177

enclosure: *"do you call this faithful?"*

if you don't cry out for help how will God come to your rescue?

This is the template of a letter I sent to 18 churches in the Greater Saint Louis Area. The sole response came from the Religious Society of Friends.

A Pledge for Your Righteous Mind

Despite being malnourished, manipulated & maligned into living an inhumane life, I pledge to remember that I am a true & righteous Human Being.

I pledge to release myself from all shame associated with the 400+ year subjugation, manipulation & de-Africanization of my ancestors, whether put on by myself or other members of society, and all related effects & defects since its inception

I pledge to be open to learning the history of my family, in order also to know myself; the history of my city, to learn how we've stood as a community, and gain insight on who I will be to all who come after me; the history of the land mass on which we stand & the corporation that "owns" it, to remember who we have always been & will become again.

I pledge to release myself and my children from the national pledge of allegiance that unknowingly bound me to an oath to serve this republic & unwillingly devote myself to a flag & to examine the negative circumstances in my life until I find their source & shine Light on them to free & heal myself.

I pledge to understand how capitalism maliciously extracts money, wealth & time from my community and to transition to spending my Black Dollars within my own communities and work toward ensuring that those Black Dollars are spent in my own communities and circulate there exhaustively before leaving.

I pledge to devote myself to becoming my highest self through discovering, knowing, and walking in my purpose & share that journey with trustworthy friends & family as I grow, with others as I mature.

I pledge allegiance to the people, to myself, and to the Divine Love that connects us all.

I accept the reality that I am still here & therefore I am one of my ancestors' strongest descendants.

I accept the reality that we are still here & therefore we are our ancestors' strongest descendants.

I accept that we must be the torchbearers, bridging the generations together, carrying forth the Light for the generations to come.

A Pledge for Your Righteous Mind
abbreviated

I pledge to remember
that I am a true and righteous Human Being.

I pledge to release myself
from all shame tied to over 400 years of subjugation.

I pledge to open myself
to learning the history of my family and myself.

I pledge to learn the history of my city
and remember who we have always been.

I pledge to release myself and my children
from any silent vows that no longer serve us.

I pledge to grow into my best self
and share my journey with those I trust.

I pledge to recognize capitalism has harmed our people
and to spend my money in ways that heal and build.

I pledge to remember I come from greatness
and carry that greatness forward.

I pledge to honor my ancestors
by building a better future for the next generation.

NOTES

_____
_____
_____
_____
_____
_____
_____
_____
_____
_____
_____
_____
_____
_____
_____
_____
_____
_____
_____
_____
_____

REFLECTIONS

authoruhtee

REFLECTIONS

POETIC REFLECTION
space to compose your own work(s) of poetry, your own psalm, your own lament, your own song

be at peace.

become love.

www.ingramcontent.com/pod-product-compliance
Lightning Source LLC
Chambersburg PA
CBHW022038090426
42741CB00007B/1118